GREEN MACHINES

ECO-TRAINS

by Golriz Golkar

Consultant: Beth Gambro
Reading Specialist, Yorkville, Illinois

Minneapolis, Minnesota

Teaching Tips

Before Reading

- Look at the cover of the book. Discuss the picture and the title.
- Ask readers to brainstorm a list of what they already know about trains. What can they expect to see in this book?
- Go on a picture walk, looking through the pictures to discuss vocabulary and make predictions about the text.

During Reading

- Read for purpose. Encourage readers to think about what makes a train an eco-train as they are reading.
- Ask readers to look for the details of the book. What are they learning about things that can make trains better for Earth?
- If readers encounter an unknown word, ask them to look at the sounds in the word. Then, ask them to look at the rest of the page. Are there any clues to help them understand?

After Reading

- Encourage readers to pick a buddy and reread the book together.
- Ask readers to name something that can make trains eco-friendly. Find the page that tells about this thing.
- Ask readers to write or draw something they learned about eco-trains.

Credits: Cover and title page, © bloodua/Getty Images; 3, © sihuo0860371/iStock; 5, © den-belitsky/iStock; 6–7, © Marco_Bonfanti/iStock; 9, © dpa picture alliance/Alamy; 10–11, © Andrew Merry/Getty Images; 13, © BeyondImages/iStock; 14–15, © cyo bo/Shutterstock; 17, © Fortgens Photography/Shutterstock; 19, © mejnak/Shutterstock; 20–21, © Kevin Foy/Alamy; 22, © brillenstimmer/Shutterstock; 23TL, © Kyodo/Newscom; 23TM, © Lee Charlie/Shutterstock; 23TR, © aapsky/iStock; 23BL, © mls-e/Shutterstock; 23BM, © TinnaPong/Shutterstock; and 23BR, © Pedal to the Stock/Shutterstock.

Library of Congress Cataloging-in-Publication Data

Names: Golkar, Golriz, author.
Title: Eco-trains / by Golriz Golkar.
Description: Minneapolis, Minnesota : Bearport Publishing Company, [2023] |
  Series: Green machines | Includes bibliographical references and index.
Identifiers: LCCN 2022002338 (print) | LCCN 2022002339 (ebook) | ISBN
  9781636917474 (library binding) | ISBN 9781636917542 (paperback) | ISBN
  9781636917610 (ebook)
Subjects: LCSH: Electric railroad trains--Juvenile literature. | Railroad
  trains--Environmental aspects--Juvenile literature. | Railroad
  trains--Technological innovations--Juvenile literature. | CYAC: Railroad
  trains. | LCGFT: Picture books. | Instructional and educational works.
Classification: LCC TF148 .G655 2023 (print) | LCC TF148 (ebook) | DDC
  625.1--dc23/eng/20220125
LC record available at https://lccn.loc.gov/2022002338
LC ebook record available at https://lccn.loc.gov/2022002339

Copyright © 2023 Bearport Publishing Company. All rights reserved. No part of this publication may be reproduced in whole or in part, stored in any retrieval system, or transmitted in any form or by any means, electronic, mechanical, photocopying, recording, or otherwise, without written permission from the publisher.

For more information, write to Bearport Publishing, 5357 Penn Avenue South, Minneapolis, MN 55419. Printed in the United States of America.

Contents

Choo, Choo! 4

Green Trains 22

Glossary 23

Index 24

Read More 24

Learn More Online 24

About the Author 24

Choo, Choo!

A train comes to a stop on the tracks.

Hop on board!

This train is special.

It is an eco-train.

Many trains use **fuel** to move.

This makes bad gases.

These gases go into the air.

They hurt Earth.

But there are other ways to make trains go.

Some eco-trains use special fuels.

These fuels do not make bad gases.

The air stays cleaner this way.

Other eco-trains use **electricity** to go.

Using electricity does not make bad gases.

Some trains use both fuel and electricity.

Say electricity like i-lek-TRIS-i-tee

Eco-trains can get electricity from a **battery**.

The battery **charges** as the train moves.

Other trains connect with cables above.

The cables give them electricity.

There are even eco-trains that use electricity and **magnets**.

Strong magnets lift and move the trains.

These trains zip along very fast.

Zoom!

Electricity from eco-trains can sometimes power other things, too.

Some trains make extra electricity.

This can go to eco-buses.

It makes the buses move.

How else are eco-trains better for Earth?

Some eco-trains can be made from old train parts.

Recycled plastic bottles and tires help make new train tracks.

Eco-trains help people travel.

They carry things to people who need them.

These trains help keep Earth clean.

Let's all go green with eco-trains!

Green Trains

Cable
Door
Track
Wheel

22

Glossary

battery something put in a machine to give it electricity

charges gives power to something

electricity a form of energy that can make things work

fuel a liquid used to make some trains go

magnets pieces of metal that can pull other metals toward them

recycled things that have been used before and are made into something new

Index

battery 12
cables 12–13, 22
electricity 10–12, 14, 16
fuel 6, 8, 10
gases 6, 8, 10
recycled 18
reused 18

Read More

Meister, Cari. *Trains (Transportation in My Community)*. North Mankato, MN: Capstone, 2019.

Wible–Freels, Korynn. *Ripley Readers Trains!* Orlando: Ripley Publishing, 2020.

Learn More Online

1. Go to **www.factsurfer.com** or scan the QR code below.
2. Enter "**Eco-Trains**" into the search box.
3. Click on the cover of this book to see a list of websites.

About the Author

Golriz Golkar loves to take electric trains to visit friends and go on family vacations.